Alphabet *of*
ANIMALS

by Laura Gates Galvin · Illustrated by Kristin Kest

SMITHSONIAN INSTITUTION

For Sarah, Alex and Isabella—the Absolute Best Cousins.—L.G.G.

To Scott with hugs from Auntie K.—K²

Book copyright © 2006 Trudy Corporation
and Smithsonian Institution, Washington, DC 20560.

Published by Soundprints, an imprint of Trudy Corporation, Norwalk, Connecticut.
www.soundprints.com

Book design: Marcin D. Pilchowski
Editors: Barbie H. Schwaeber and Ben Nussbaum

First Paperback Edition 2008
10 9 8 7 6 5 4 3 2 1
Printed in China

Acknowledgments:
     Our very special thanks to the following curators for their careful review of this book: Dr. Gary R. Graves
of the Division of Vertebrate Zoology, Dr. George Zug and Dr. Don E. Wilson of the Department of Systematic
Biology, and Dr. Gary Hevel of the Department of Entomology, all part of Smithsonian Institution's National
Museum of Natural History.
     Soundprints would also like to thank Ellen Nanney and Katie Mann at Smithsonian Institution's Office of
Product Development and Licensing for their help in the creation of this book.

ISBN 978-1-59249-991-5 (pbk.)

The Library of Congress Cataloging-in-Publication Data below applies only to the hardcover edition of this book.

Library of Congress Cataloging-in-Publication Data

Galvin, Laura Gates

     Alphabet of animals / by Laura Gates Galvin ; edited by Ben Nussbaum.—1st ed.
        p. cm.—(Smithsonian alphabet books)
     ISBN 1-59249-655-5 (hardcover)
     1. Animals—Juvenile literature. 2. English language—Alphabet—Juvenile
     literature. I. Nussbaum, Ben. II. Title. III. Series.
     QL49.G2415 2006
     590—dc22
                                          2006014864

Alphabet *of*
ANIMALS

by Laura Gates Galvin   **Illustrated by Kristin Kest**

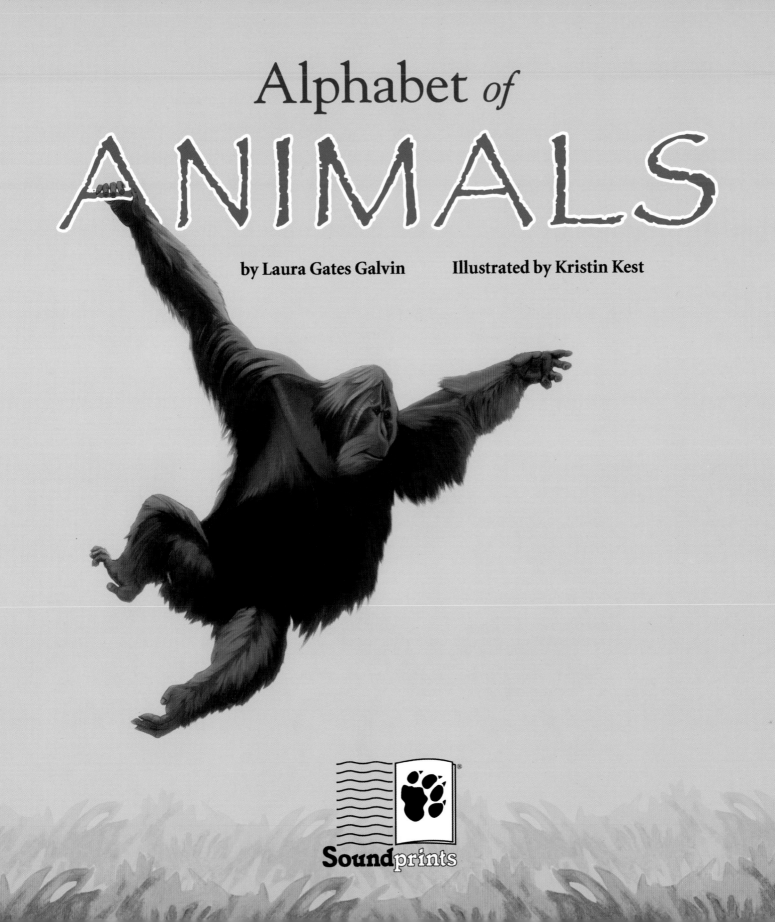

Soundprints

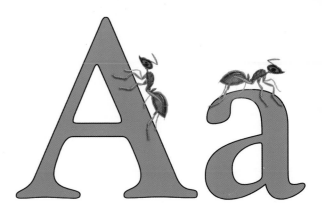

A is for **ant**
with a nest underground.
She is tiny but strong.
She can move things around.

Bb

B is for **blue-footed booby**.
Her feet are bright blue.
She has a sharp bill
and lives in Peru.

C is for **coyote**.
His fur is light brown.
He runs very fast
with his tail pointed down.

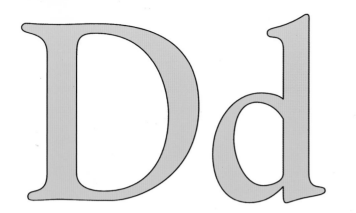

D is for **deer**.
Some have white puffy tails.
The big sets of antlers
are just on the males.

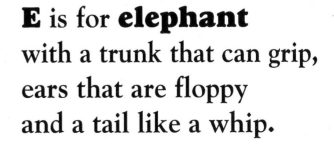

E is for **elephant**
with a trunk that can grip,
ears that are floppy
and a tail like a whip.

Ff

F is for **flamingo** taking a drink. The food that she eats makes her turn pink.

Gg

G is for **giraffe**
with a neck that is long.
She pulls leaves from treetops
with a tongue that is strong.

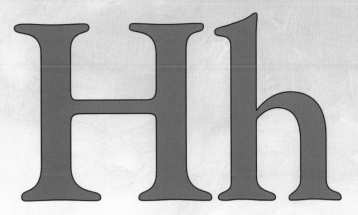

Hh

H is for **hippo**.
He enjoys being wet.
He's in water all day
and on land at sunset.

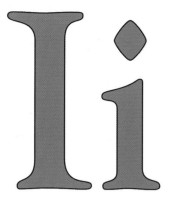

I is for **iguana**.
His skin can be green.
He may look quite fierce,
but he's not at all mean.

J is for **jackrabbit**.
He's eating his lunch.
Sagebrush and grass
are what he likes to munch.

Jj

Kk

K is for **kangaroo.**
She hops on two feet.
She carries her joey,
so little and sweet.

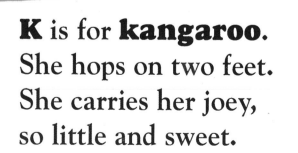

L is for **lemur**
with eyes big and round.
Madagascar, near Africa,
is where they are found.

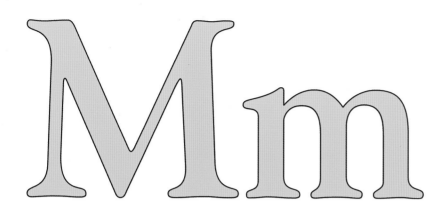

M is for **mouse.**
She is furry and small.
When people are close
she hides near a wall.

Nn

N is for **newt** hiding under a log. He's an amphibian just like a frog!

Oo

O is for **orangutan**.
He is big and strong.
He has fingers and toes
and arms that are long.

P is for **porcupine**.
She has many skills,
like protecting herself
by using her quills.

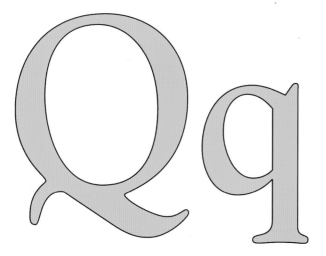

Q is for **queen bee**
laying eggs in her nest.
She's always so busy—
no time for a rest!

R is for **raccoon.**
He makes a loud crash,
while looking for food
inside of the trash!

Ss

S is for **skunk**
who sleeps in the day.
She protects herself
with her stinky spray.

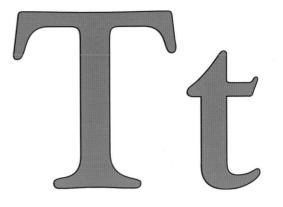

T t

T is for **tortoise**
taking a rest.
A cool shady spot
is where he likes best.

Uu

U is for **umbrellabird**
with feathers so big
on top of his head
like a big, floppy wig.

V is for **vampire bat** gliding in the night. He has sharp little teeth and a strange appetite!

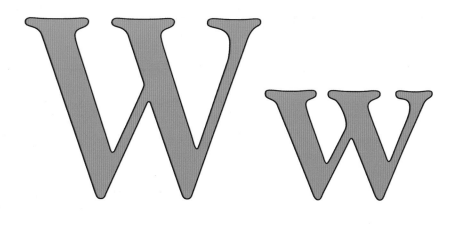

W is for **warthog**.
She's a big wild pig.
She looks for her food
using her snout to dig.

X x

X is for **xantus hummingbird**
a delicate bird.
Stay very quiet
so her hum can be heard.

Yy

Y is for **yak**
standing in a storm.
He doesn't get cold.
His coat keeps him warm!

Z is for **zebra**.
She has striped fur.
Her stripes make a pattern
that's unique just to her.

GLOSSARY

ANT: The ant shown in this book is a little black ant—little black ant is actually a specific species—it can be black or brown. Little black ants live in underground nests. There is usually a small mound of dirt at the entrance to the nests. These common ants also nest in rotten wood. The workers can be seen night and day carrying morsels of food to their nest mates.

BLUE-FOOTED BOOBY: The blue-footed booby is an unusual-looking tropical seabird with webbed feet similar to a duck's—but unlike a duck's feet, they are bright blue in color. When blue-footed boobies are on land, they are quite clumsy. They are also tame and unafraid of predators. The name "booby" is a very fitting name for this seabird, because in Spanish it translates to "stupid fellow"—the blue-footed booby is not one of the smartest birds! Blue-footed boobies live in the Galapagos Islands and they can be found in the coastal region of Ecuador, northern Peru and on the west coast of Mexico.

COYOTE: Coyotes are dog-like animals that live alone in a mated pair, or with a small pack. One way to tell the coyote apart from wolves and dogs is to watch its tail when it runs. The coyote runs with its tail down. Dogs run with their tails up and wolves run with their tails straight out. Coyotes can be found in the Western Hemisphere from the Pacific to Atlantic Oceans.

DEER: The deer depicted in this book is a white-tailed deer. The white-tailed deer can be found in southern Canada and most of the United States, except for the Southwest, Alaska and Hawaii. Male deer have antlers. They shed them between January and March. New antlers will grow again in April or May and will have a soft covering, called velvet, on them. The antlers will lose the velvet in August or September.

ELEPHANT: Elephants are extremely intelligent animals. They are also the largest land animals, weighing up to 12,000 pounds! Elephant trunks are very strong and they have many uses, including smelling, eating, drinking and gripping. Elephants even use their trunks to hold on to each other's tails—it's like an elephant's way of holding hands!

FLAMINGO: Flamingos are very exotic-looking birds with feathers that range in color from light pink to red, depending on the species. Flamingos eat small crustaceans, brine, shrimp and aquatic plants. Flamingo diets are very high in beta-carotene, which is what makes their feathers pink.

GIRAFFE: The giraffe is the tallest animal in the world, measuring 16 to 18 feet tall. Its favorite meal is the thorny leaves of the acacia tree. The giraffe uses its very strong tongue to pull the leaves from the trees. The giraffe is so tall that it can easily spot predators. In the wild, giraffes live about 25 years.

HIPPOPOTAMUS: The hippo spends its day wading in shallow water. Sometimes hundreds of hippos will share a small patch of water. The hippo's night begins a few hours after sunset, when all the hippos file out of the water to graze on the land.

IGUANA: The iguana depicted in this book is a green iguana. Green iguanas, not surprisingly, are green in color. However, they can be found in many different shades of green and gray. Green iguanas reach 4 to 6 feet in length as adults and they have long fingers and toes and sharp claws to help them climb and grasp. The green iguana occurs in tropical lowlands from Mexico to southern Brazil and Paraguay.

JACKRABBIT: Jackrabbits are technically hares, not rabbits. The main difference is that hares give birth and raise their young above ground. Baby hares are born fully furred, with their eyes wide open. Hares are strict vegetarians, eating a great variety of herbs and shrubs.

KANGAROO: The kangaroo is a common marsupial from the islands of Australia and New Guinea. A baby kangaroo is called a joey. When they are born, each joey is the size of a jellybean, and it is blind and hairless. A joey lives in its mother's pouch for the first year, and then stays close to its mother so it can learn from her. Kangaroos are the only large mammals that can hop.

LEMUR: Lemurs are found only in Madagascar (an island off the coast of Africa) and the neighboring Comores Islands. On these islands, lemurs live in a variety of habitats. Some live in moist, tropical rainforests, while others live in dry desert areas. The lemur is a kind of primate, which means it is related to apes and humans.

MOUSE: The mouse depicted in this book is a deer mouse. The deer mouse is one of the most common of the small mammals. The deer mouse's tail helps it balance when climbing. Although deer mice are primarily found in wooded areas, they will occasionally enter buildings, particularly during the winter.

NEWT: Newts are a type of salamander that live in water and on land. Newts are amphibians, as are frogs and toads. There are about a dozen different species of newts, one in the eastern U.S., two in the western U.S., and the rest in Northern Africa and Europe. Often mistaken for lizards, newts have moist skin. They have no scales, claws or external ear openings.

ORANGUTAN: Orangutans can be found in tropical rain forests in Asia. Orangutans are large apes that can walk on two feet like humans. However, they rarely walk—instead, they use their strong arms to swing from branch to branch, tree to tree. Except for mothers and babies, orangutans live alone in a wide territory of trees. They eat and sleep in the trees—they even drink in the trees, finding water in hollows. Orangutans have hands and feet that are very similar to humans, each with five fingers and five toes.

PORCUPINE: The porcupine is a member of the rodent family. The front half of the porcupine's body is covered in long guard hairs. Its backside and tail are covered in over 30,000 quills. When under attack, the porcupine lashes out with its spiny tail. Porcupines cannot throw their quills, although the quills are easily dislodged when the porcupine shakes its tail, which may give the impression that the quills are being thrown.

QUEEN BEE: The queen bee lays eggs that hatch into thousands of young bees. Laying eggs is the queen's only function. She does not gather food or build a honeycomb. Queen bees can live for 3 to 4 years and may lay up to 2,000 eggs per day. Queen bees live for an average of three years, while worker bees have an average life span of only three months.

RACCOON: A raccoon is very intelligent and very curious. It has a black mask that stretches across the eyes and black rings around the tail. The raccoon has slender human-like hands that allow it to move around quickly and easily. Because of their intelligence and ability to adapt, many raccoons can be found in urban areas.

SKUNK: The skunk is similar in size to a housecat. The unique characteristic of the skunk is its ability to spray a foul-smelling oily musk when it encounters danger. Animals that are close to the skunk get fluid in their eyes, causing intense pain and a brief loss of vision. The skunk can be found throughout the interior and southern Canadian provinces and in all of the United States.

TORTOISE: Tortoises are reptiles that live on land and eat fruits, flowers and vegetables. Tortoises do not have webbed feet. Their hind feet are round and stumpy (like elephant feet) for walking on land.

UMBRELLABIRD: The umbrellabird is a bird that lives in warm, humid South and Central American rain forests. The umbrellabird gets its name from the crest feathers on its head that rise above its bill and fan out like an umbrella. These feathers are more noticeable in males than in females. The male umbrellabird also has a long skin wattle on its neck that inflates like a small balloon when the bird booms, or makes its vocal sounds.

VAMPIRE BAT: At night, the vampire bat emerges from dark caves, tree hollows, and abandoned buildings in Mexico and Central and South America. The vampire bat gets its food by drinking the blood of other animals for survival. It feeds on blood from cows, pigs and horses. The blood feeding is done through a small wound and does not hurt the animal.

WARTHOG: The warthog is a wild pig that can be found in Africa. The warthog looks fierce, but it often avoids fighting predators by running away or dodging into a burrow. Warthogs can run up to 30 miles an hour, often outdistancing a pursuer.

XANTUS HUMMINGBIRD: Xantus hummingbirds live in Baja California along the Pacific Coast. The male hummingbird is beautifully colored — he has a bluish-black face, a metallic green throat, a black and white stripe on the side of its head and a red bill with a black tip. Xantus hummingbirds build their nests in trees from plant fibers, spider silk and other soft material.

YAK: The wild yak lives high among the snow-covered mountains of Tibet. Its thick skin and long shaggy coat, which almost reaches the ground, protect it from the bitter cold. Its coat is so thick and warm that the yak can sleep comfortably directly on the snow. The yak is a very agile mountain climber. It can easily cover great distances throughout its rocky homeland.

ZEBRA: The zebra is a member of the horse family. It has excellent hearing and eyesight and can run at speeds of up to 35 miles per hour. Different zebra species have different types of stripes, from narrow to wide. In fact, the farther south on the African plains you travel, the farther apart the stripes on the zebras get. No two zebras have the same pattern of stripes, just like no two people have the same fingerprints!

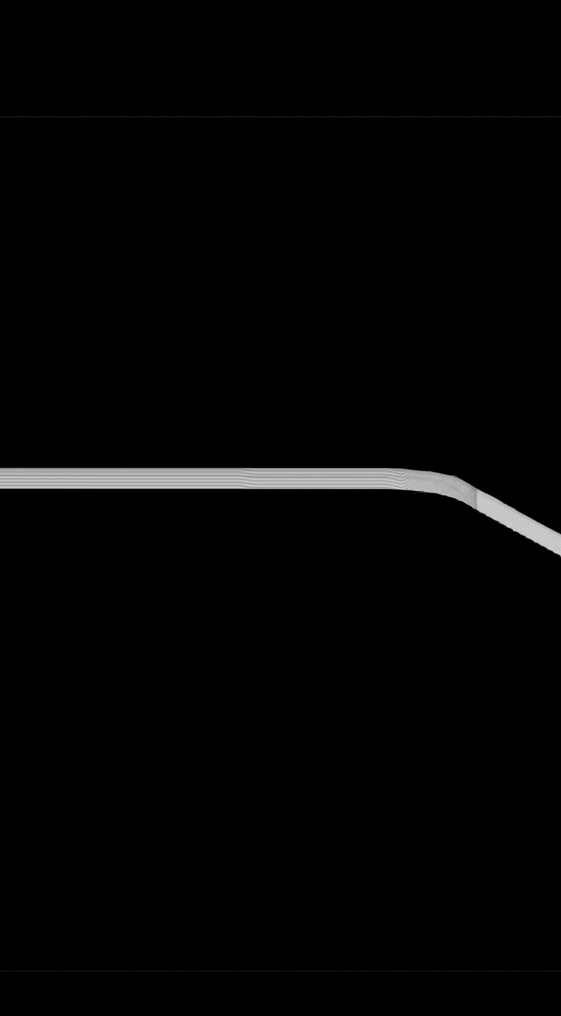

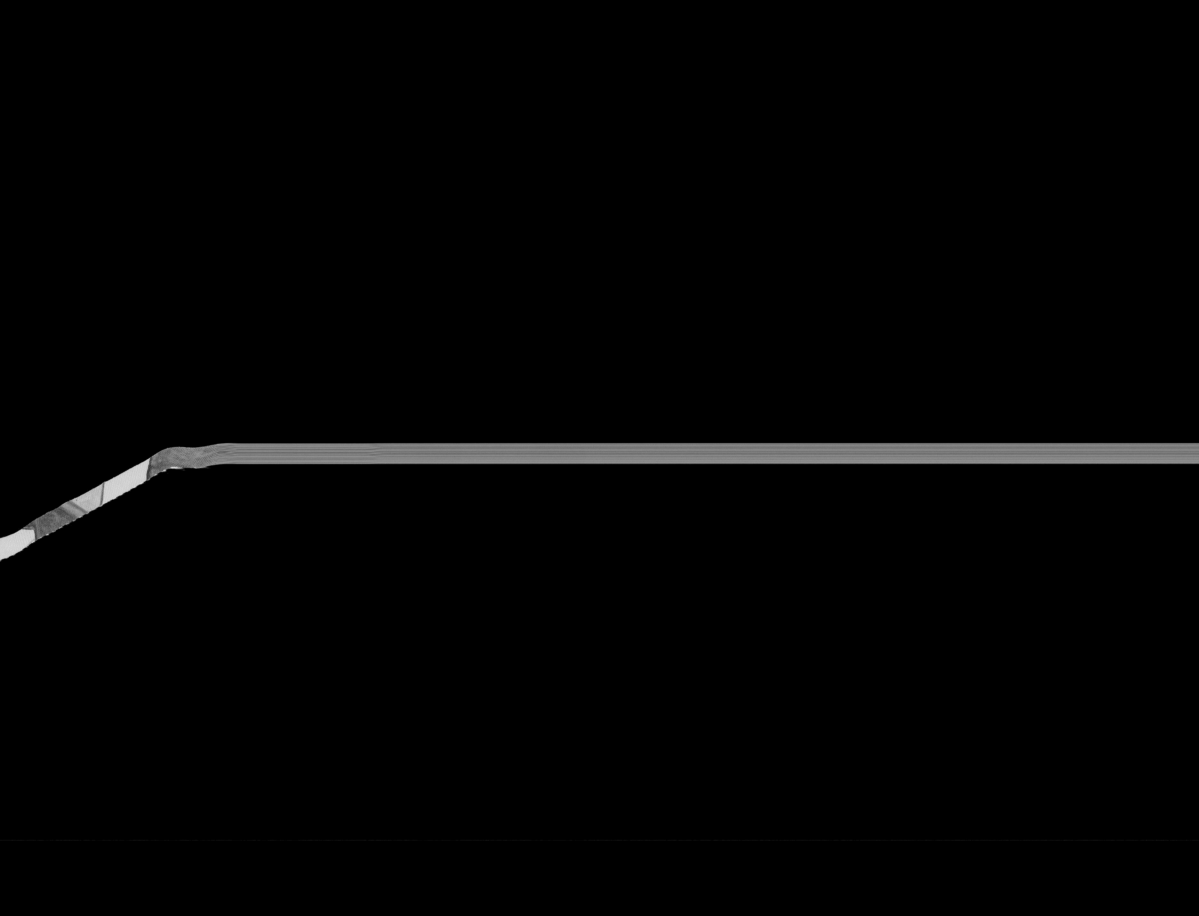